UNSPOKEN WORD
Love, Longing & Letting Go

✳ ❊ ❋

ADVANCED PRAISE

"Your poetry has given me one of the greatest gifts of all — hope."
– Michael Nouri, Television and Film Actor

"*Unspoken Word* is entrancing — a stellar accomplishment. This precious book is a rare treasure, a cloudburst of wisdom, a true feast for the soul."
– John Audette, Author, *Loved by the Light: True Stories of Divine Intervention and Providence*

"Mitch's poetry resonates with the story of my life and pours forth like an erupting volcano, igniting that unnameable thirst within."
– Joan Apter, Healer and Author, *Miracle of Thirst*

"Ditkoff connects everything with invisible threads of joy that point to a past, present and future of profound acceptance and gratitude for what is."
– Rabbi Zoe B. Zak, Temple Israel, Catskill, New York

"I spent a month reading a few poems each day from *Unspoken Word*. It became a journey of searching my own soul. It connected me with my loved ones, the world, and a better understanding of myself."
– Hank Alpert, President, Spartan Petroleum Corp.

"I've just read the first few poems and am very touched. Tears started falling almost immediately. How beautiful! For me, what you've written is a love letter I want to savor."
– Susan Hubly, Realtor

"Mitch Ditkoff's poems are striking and lyrical. His wide range of poetic styles reflect the gentle romanticism of Rilke and Gibran and the wry wit of Billy Collins. Like Rumi and Hafiz, Mitch has the gift of distilling infinity into words that inspire you to feel its vastness within you."
– Francisca Matos, Writer

"Inspiring. Ecstatic. Mystical. Profound. Exciting. Mesmerizing. Juicy. Memorable. Joyous. Wondrous. Sublime. Uplifting."
– Jonathan Lloyd, Writer & TaiChi/QiGong teacher

"Mitch Ditkoff's poetry is inspired. His writing makes the unseen world visible and palpable. It opens the heart."
– Stevie Ray McHugh, Author, *You Are God Enough*

"*Unspoken Word* evokes some of my favorite devotional poets, Rumi in particular. These pages will delight with a familiarity similar to remembering an enchanting dream that has long been forgotten."
– MaryAnne Erickson, Fine Artist

"From the very first poem in this book, we find ourselves on a journey all of us share in common. Mitch Ditkoff has eloquently put into words the transcendence of our limitations as we experience the grace of being human."
– Steve Ornstein, Founder, Israel Seen

"If one thinks of ecstatic poetry as something created in the past and pre-served by a few in the present, I offer another possibility. Make way for the living! Mitch Ditkoff lives in his own ecstatic landscape — *now*. He reminds us of this magical place we all share because we are alive."
– Alla Rogers, Director of Art and Cultural Impact Programs, Global Peace Education Network

"Mitch Ditkoff takes us on the ride of our lives, holding us tenderly and showing us what's possible in the world and in ourselves.
Unspoken Word is a gift!"
– Joseph Bennett, Author, *Rest, The Art of Doing Less*

"These beautiful poems reflect us back to ourselves, allowing us to see our human condition with greater love and compassion, to breathe a sigh of relief and flow."
– Ellen Goldberg, Mystic and Author, *The Art and Science of Hand Reading*

"I applaud Mitch's relentless efforts to share these secrets of the heart, for they are hints of how to enter through that invisible door to your truest home."
– Jan Buchalter, Humanitarian

"One cannot fail to respond to the call of Mitch's poetry to awaken us in the midst of life's circumstances. No matter how apparently estranged from our hearts we feel or troubled in mind, we glance a second time at what's before us and find it suddenly transformed."
– Robert Esformes, Cantor

"*The world is an illusion, but you have to act as if it's real.*"
– Krishna

"*Here's the new rule: break the wineglass
and fall towards the glassblower's breath.*"
– Rumi

"*If there's a book that you want to read, but it hasn't been written yet,
then you must write it.*"
– Toni Morrison

Dedicated to Prem Rawat

Published in the United States by:
    Idea Champions Press, 268 Main Street, Catskill, NY 12414
Cover Illustration: Tim Gainey, https://hazysunimages.com

Ditkoff, Mitchell
UNSPOKEN WORD: Love, Longing & Letting Go
ISBN: 978-0-9969122-5-9
1. Poetry

TABLE OF CONTENTMENT

TWO

THREE

FOUR

FIVE

✳ ❄ ✺

NOTE FROM THE AUTHOR

Welcome to *Unspoken Word*. I'm glad you have made it this far. The fact that you are holding my book in your hands is not an accident. It means something – or could mean something – that is, if you choose to keep reading, an activity that has become increasingly rare these days. Especially when it comes to poetry. Poetry is way down on the list of what people read in the 21st century – well behind tweets, Instagram messages, and the backs of cereal boxes.

I'm not surprised. For most of us, our introduction to poetry was either painful or boring – something we were forced to pay attention to in high school by a teacher who probably should have retired a long time ago. Like most people, we assume poetry is stuffy, elitist, or dense. Well, maybe some of it is, but hopefully not the poems in this book. I've done my best to make them pop. And besides, you have some momentum now. You are already into your second paragraph.

Think of the poetry you are about to read as a sanctuary – a place to pause, ponder, and feel something just a little bit different than usual. Please don't feel compelled to read all of it in one sitting. There is no rush. No one is keeping score. Go as slow as you want and savor what you read like you would an ice cream cone on a summer day.

When you're done with the book, you might want to prop open a window with it or give it to a friend. The main thing? Enjoy it! And, even more importantly, enjoy yourself. You are a miracle.

Mitch Ditkoff
April 10, 2023
Catskill, New York, USA

UNSPOKEN WORD

Love
Longing
& Letting Go

MITCH DITKOFF

WHY I WROTE THIS BOOK

I wrote this book for the same reasons flowers bloom.

There is a force of nature within me that begs to be expressed. It's as simple as that. It takes many shapes, this life-giving, creative energy. It has many moods, many moves, many moons. On a good day, I let it have its way with me, taking its hand and going where it leads, praying I don't get in the way of what's wanting to be said.

"Poetry," explained Leonard Cohen, "is just the evidence of life. If your life is burning well, poetry is just the ash."

And there you have it, my friends. Ashes to ashes, dust to dust – while we warm ourselves and dance around the fire of our lives.

My hope? That the poetry of *Unspoken Word* will serve you in some way – nurturing, enlivening, delighting, inspiring, awakening, and helping you open the extraordinary gift that is your life.

If you like, think of my poetry as the hieroglyphics of my heart translated into English by the wonder and gratitude I feel by simply being alive.

ONE

*"It is only with the heart that one can see rightly;
what is essential is invisible to the eye."*

– Antoine de Saint Exupery

The Gift

The gift
I bought
for you
today
is not
inside
the box.
It's in
the opening.

Some Might Call It Dancing

Some might call it dancing,
I call it stumbling closer to God,
the unrehearsed falling forward into love
as if the world was tipped.

May I Stay Here Forever?

May I stay here forever
in this perfect place of peace with you –
the sacred space between in breath and out,
the final coming home,
timeless moment before the need
for anything has risen,
Buddha enjoying his late afternoon nap
with no one around to extract any meaning from it.

First, there is a breath,
and then, there is a second.

This is how I begin my long walk with you
by the water's edge,
cool white sand beneath both our feet.

The One for Whom You Create

Poets, lose your pens,
painters, toss your brushes in the sea,
musicians, give your instruments away,
then go for a long walk.
When you're done,
keep walking,
notice the beauty all around you,
do not try to remember a thing.
breathe,
this holy moment is your poetry,
your art, your song,
do not concern yourself with giving it form,
the one for whom you create
deeply loves what you just didn't do.

Here's the Problem with Reading Rumi

Here's the problem with reading Rumi:
there's a good chance you will never come back,
which might, of course, be fine for you, oh seeker of light,
but what about the person
you are most committed to here on planet Earth?
Won't they feel abandoned,
you having disappeared without a trace,
your body now a shadow,
your heart having exploded into a thousand pieces,
each one a seed about to populate another world?

What about *that* person,
the one you share your hopes and dreams with,
the one who holds you late at night?

If this is what concerns you, my friend,
please tell your partner this:
Oh my dearest darling, if only I knew who I was,
I would sing to you all night and day,
which is why, you see, I read Rumi, the pied piper of my soul.

He is the one who opens me up to what life is really about.

You and I, my dear, are more than just a couple,
we are couplets in a greater poem,
each one a moving line with its own rhythm
and internal rhyme,
expressions of the ancient quest for love
now made greater by each other,
why I come home to you at night,
why you come home to me,
why I must forgive myself daily for forgetting
just how divine you are, sweet bee to the honey of my life –
the endless sky I soar deeper into stretching my wings
beyond what I know,
and it's all Rumi's fault.

Blame him!
I had nothing to do with it.
Nothing!

They Are Still Laughing

I had 100% control of my mind
for a moment or two –
the work of a thousand lifetimes
hiding in a dark forest,
then I let go.
It had nothing to do with enlightenment,
my sudden release. No,
it was more like the dropping
of a heavy bag of rocks.
The splash it made
in the still waters below
cooled a few small children.

They are still laughing.

This Thirst

There is an aching deep within my heart
that cannot be explained.
It wakes me in the middle of the night
and write these lines –
a kind of fishing in a great sea I cannot find by day.

This escapade is not the search for something new,
it is not the need to find –
more it is the being *moved*,
my being pulled by an unseen moon,
how small birds, when days get cold, make their way
across dark skies to the place where they were born,
how a feather falls to earth
and a child, finding it, looks up,
why dogs pace back and forth before a door
as their master turns for home.

Ah, this restlessness, this thirst, this ache,
this silent undertow inside
that takes me back to the hidden spring
where lions come to drink,
and snakes,
why birds sing when they are all alone
and the long ride home on an empty train
often feels like an arrival.

Rilke's Late Night Violin Music

Rainer Maria Rilke, the genius German poet
who translated God in ways
no scripture ever can,
once wondered why every time he walked
beneath a high window
(out of which violin music could be heard)
he thought it promised him a future lover.

When I go to the great beyond, I want to meet this man,
standing, as I imagine he will be, just beyond
the gathering of my long-gone relatives waiting for me.
I don't think he will be saying much of anything,
just looking in my general direction, his dark eyes singing,
his body completely at ease, having just released
a thousand poems he never needed to write,
the lips of his high-windowed lovers still unkissed,
summoned as they were by violins to embrace him
far beyond the body's few pleasures.

Rilke will not be looking up,
remembering as he was, from a few years ago,
that beautiful young couple crossing the street before him,
laughing, holding hands, but not his glance,
always reserved, it seemed, for somebody else,
but if you dared to ask "for whom?"
he would fumble for his pen,
reach inside the quiet pocket of his favorite coat,
and find the old notebook he always kept there
for precisely moments
like this.

How To Listen to the Beloved

First of all,
give up everything you know
about listening –
it has nothing to do with your ears,
that kind of listening
will only take you so far.
If you really want to hear,
you will need to leave your ears at the door
and while you're at it,
your head,
then take a seat,
breathe deep,
let go and become,
if you can,
a flower opening to the sun.

The Real Marriage

Today, my own best man, alone in my room,
I am going to marry myself,
love who I am until death do me part,
embracing what exists at the core of my being,
knowing, as I do, that my soul mate lives inside me,
closer than my own breath,
muse of my muse and has always been with me,
even when I was not, whole until itself,
radiant, free,
snuggling in its wrinkled pajamas with infinity.

This marriage of myself,
this loving the love that loves
is not a rejection of the world,
nor is it a denial of the passionate glory of loving another,
it is, quite simply,
the recognition that who and what I am
were made for each other a long time ago,
best friends, lovers,
the pauses in this poem,
not so much holding hands,
but being held in the massive arms
of the nameless One who animates us all.

This Feeling Inside Me

The tears of a thousand lifetimes searching for you
is the ocean I sail upon today,
stunned with the knowledge that both of us are alive,
but far too many miles apart.

Wind in my sails, I see the sun,
the sky, and the backs of my own hands,
having aged, it seems, when I wasn't looking,
odd little brown spots some kind of secret code
I do not understand.

This feeling inside me,
this uncontainable, untranslatable feeling inside me
is all I am today,
my heart, a helium-filled child's balloon,
flying free.

Overhead, I see a seagull,
just one,
wings outstretched,
having caught the updraft
and gliding.

Silenced

Now that I've seen what creates me,
I no longer need to die
or speak of moon-risen eyes
of others gone wild for me.

Amazed, I stand alone now
at the sight of the one
who lightens the stones
and tunes my ear to the sound of my own heart
no longer locked behind bones.

Outside,
leaves are turning the color of old men's teeth
and I blush at the thought
of ever really being alone with you.

How can I explain?

Driftwood here I have become,
carried to a shore beyond my sight,
cave of undiscovered gold,
pure earth,
first ray of sun,
moonbeam in the slow night of my arrival.

An Ode to Self-Improvement

If you are trying to improve yourself,
please take a moment to consider the possibility
that the self you are trying to improve
either does not exist
or is totally self-invented
and what you are really trying to do
is improve your persona,
the wind-up doll of yourself that you have conjured up
to make your way forward in the world,
an understandable past-time, indeed,
but not the real purpose of life.

And, just to make matters even more interesting,
who is it that's trying? Who?
Upon what ground is that person standing
and why are they trying so hard?

Is there really something wrong with you?
And, if so, who is judging whom?
Maybe *that's* the self that needs to be improved.

Just for the moment, consider the possibility
that life is not a matter of self-improvement.
Maybe it's more a matter of knowing yourself.
Perhaps once this so-called self is known,
there will be no more need for self-improvement.
Wouldn't that be interesting?
Imagine what you could do with all that extra time!
Think about what a big, beautiful space would open up for you –
kind of like one of those fields Rumi liked to wander in.

With all that newly found time in your life
maybe you could take up gardening
or learn to play the piano,
or maybe you could just make someone a cup of tea.

Like yourself, for example.

My Uber Driver

My Uber driver, I just found out,
sings in a Mexican rock band,
80's covers, Spanish only.
That's why he asks me to sit in the front seat with him today.

If I sit in the back, he explains,
the State Police will impound his grey Toyota
and he'll never get to gig again.
They will keep his car for two months behind a barbed wire fence
next to a field where many dogs bark.
35,000 pesos it will cost him if he ever wants to see
his vehiculo again.
As it turns out, the Regional Governor
owns the local taxi company, 100 shiny green and white cabs.

That's why the State Police, in leather boots,
stops Uber drivers in my little town,
but only if their passengers are sitting in the back seat.
Not today, however.
Today, I am sitting in the front seat
like Pablo's best friend.

Here's How I Want To Love You

Here's how I want to love you:
as if both of us had just been told
we only had a week to live.
I would hold you,
stroke your hair and sing,
each cell in my body
throwing open its fabulous doors to the sky
and the great emancipation of your soul.
You would breathe and I would, too,
each breath savored,
your eyes portals to the other side,
my long looking at you
a large field we now find ourselves dancing in.

After Listening to You

After listening to you,
I am moving much differently today,
more like the wind than one on his way,
more like the river with nothing to say,
more like the prayer than needing to pray.
How this transformation happens is a mystery to me,
I do nothing, but have everything, I work and I play.
I seek nothing, but find,
sitting alone in the room of myself, a newly crowned king.
My heart is a milkweed and you are the breeze,
me standing taller now that I'm down on my knees,
receiver of a fortune I never knew was mine –
one that's been waiting for me since the beginning of time –
my need to count gone, the long journey done.

You see, and you do,
I have nothing to measure and nothing to measure it with
here in this place of pure being, breathing pure pleasure.

Can it really be this simple? Can it really be
that after all these years of searching for the holy grail
the holy grail is me?
Maybe that's why babies smile and old monks laugh,
maybe that's why the two of us are one,
you my better half.

Some people get this on their death bed,
some by almost dying, some know it from their birth,
some get lost in trying.

Today, a thousand psalms fill my cells
and I listen to the silence before a single word is sung.
How simple life is! There is no bell to ring, nowhere to go,
nothing to bring, no seed to sow.
The flag is not moving, nor is the wind
here in this place where a thousand, grateful angels
find themselves dancing on the head of a pin.

What Is This Strange Forgetting?

What is this strange forgetting
that has taken hold of me lately –
this being unable to remember
that everything is
sacred, holy, and alive?
The absence of you, my Friend,
surely has something to do with it,
your being gone has opened
a small hole in me, a pinprick,
the kind blood brothers make,
but you are nowhere in sight.

Where are you?
Something is leaving me slowly,
there's a leak I cannot see.
A day's worth amounts to almost nothing,
a week's would barely fill a thimble,
but it's been months now without you
and I am starting to notice,
lurking like a stranger in my own shadow
and sleeping just a little too long.

Hey! I've got an idea!
Why don't you cross the universe today,
and show up unannounced at my door?
I can't wait to see
the looks on the faces of my friends
who have been so diligently reminding me,
these past few days,
that you are already here.

Harvest Me

Stories of your beauty
drift down to me like ash
from a fire
I have not yet been warmed by.
Your absence only singes me
and though I flame at the mere mention of you,
still I remain unconsumed.
Don't you understand?
Just the wind of your walking
would be enough to release me,
your reaching,
enough to wake me from this dream.

There Is No Door

I could tell you that my Master
is the one who opened the door,
but that would be a lie,
there never was a door,
I was never on the other side –
we were always in this together, he and I.

If you call the realization of this oneness,
the opening of a door,
then I guess we have the beginning of a very long poem here,
but since I'm in a really good mood today,
I'll save you the trouble of hacking your way
through a love drunk's excess of metaphors.

There is no door!
Never was, never will be.
The knocking you hear
is only the sound of your own heart beating.

The One for whom it beats has always been with you,
so what's all this monkey business about a door?

The Only Pilgrimage Required

Here's a little secret:
every breath you take is a prayer,
22,000 times a day
it rises, unannounced,
then returns to who knows where,
you do not need to kneel,
you do not need to speak,
and the only pilgrimage required
is the one from head to heart,
the one all people seek.

Two

"One can have no smaller or greater mastery then mastery of oneself."
– Leonardo DaVinci

It's All Foreplay

It's all foreplay,
every single thing you do
or don't,
each glance, each breath,
the way you turn your head
or walk across a room,
no one there to notice,
every flower planted,
picked or twirled,
every pirouette.

It's all foreplay,
all of it,
every single thing,
the way you pause,
and check the time,
the way you don't,
unsure if the perfume
through your half-opened window is for you,
the scent of someone else's skin,
the way you close your eyes,
the oh so slow anticipation
that precedes absolutely everything,
incense lit, thin wisps of smoke
disappearing into a night
no one wants to end,
blinking, breathing,
beholding the unbearable beauty of simply being alive,
the touch of a hand,
the thought of a rose,
the way you reach for something you don't really need.

Who Can I Share My Joy With?

Who can I share my joy with?
Who can understand?
My body is the hourglass,
my breath the precious sand.

Pavarotti and I

Luciano Pavarotti just walked into my kitchen.
He is crying,
not for all those arias that made their way through him
when he was a much younger man,
but the ones not yet written,
the joy of a thousand composers still unborn.

He asks me if I have a clove of garlic,
which I am glad to say, I do, and toss it to him,
amazed at how large a man he is.
He finds the knife, himself,
humming as he makes his way across the room
and begins chopping, slowly at first
and then with great abandon,
almost as if the 10 million people he has performed for
were all in the room with us, which they are,
hearts bursting
like unpicked pomegranates beneath a Tuscan sun.

Pavarotti, I am happy to say, keeps on chopping,
even when I think, for the third time,
the pieces are small enough
for the sauce he won't begin to make
until all my neighbors are asleep.

We ate well that night, Luciano and I,
we laughed and drank a lot of wine.

He told me a story about the time
he was way too drunk to sing
in a country he couldn't quite remember.

The Paradox Supreme

Here is the paradox supreme:
what you want you have
and what you have you want,
what you call the path
is merely the way to this understanding,
do not worry about the first step,
you have already taken it.

If You Want To Love Me

If you want to love me,
love yourself first,
if you want to love yourself first,
love me.
When you understand this, oh precious one,
everything will begin to make sense,
all doors will open
all windows, all hearts, all minds,
nothing left to own but yourself,
nowhere else to go,
you having arrived a long time ago.

Here's as simple as it gets:
love is the center of the universe,
everything revolves around it.
Einstein understood this,
one of the reasons, no doubt,
he always seemed to be on the verge
of something or other,
his hair the only proof he needed,
that and his love for the violin.
But, if perchance, you should ever lose your way,
the original orbit you came here with
and find yourself
drifting into the far reaches of space, no one to hold you,
know this:
every cell in your body is a standing ovation before God,
let them all sing out,
let the massive choruses of joy and longing within you
fully express themselves,
understand, without thinking,
that everything, exactly as it is now, is perfect,
a gift.

Face Your Life Like a Cuban Trumpet Player

Face your life
like a Cuban trumpet player
standing his ground
for whatever comes next,
eyes straight ahead,
not a thought in the world
and blowing,
I said blowing his horn
at the peak of his power
so his long-gone grandfather,
the man who worked the sugar cane fields
and always had a kind word for strangers,
can hear.

The Width of the Universe

Astrophysicists claim the universe is 94 billion light years wide,
please don't ask me how they know, I can't tell you,
especially since the half-life of scientific knowledge,
these days, is only five years,
meaning that 50% of what Earth's wisest believe to be true
will be proven false a year from now.
OK, so maybe the universe isn't 94 billion light years wide,
or maybe there isn't just one universe, maybe there are many,
what's been called, the multiverse, for lack of a better word,
kind of like this poem if I

left a large enough space between verses

or maybe the whole concept of distance
is completely old school, like penmanship or Ritz crackers
and, in reality, nothing exists except *this moment*
or, as my father used to say,
"that and $2.50 will get you on the subway."

The point of it all? Love!
Love is the name of the game.
Love and kindness and compassion and forgiveness
and gratitude and, of course, consciousness,
speaking of which,
the most advanced space craft ever reverse-engineered
from another world had no moving parts,
no dials, no dashboard, no grommets, no chips, no nothing.

It was powered *by consciousness alone*,
the mind waves of the beings who traveled inside it.

And this, my friends, is precisely why I love baseball so much,
the shortstop doesn't give a shit about how wide the universe is,
and the center fielder, he of the big biceps and rugged good looks,
has just hit a 468-foot home run into the upper deck.
Now that's far.

I Want to Say Thank You

I want to say thank you, but to whom?
Who am I grateful to,
the one for whom I was born
or should I say born through,
the source of it all,
the center of the wheel,
the hub?
Who?

Who is it, this one,
this holy, ever present one?

Do you know, my friend?
Do you know the space between each breath,
the healer of your broken heart,
the ancient one,
gracious beyond death,
your parents gone or going,
your heroes, lovers, friends
and all those unremembered words
whispered slowly in the dark,
the best of you driftwood on the far shore of arrival,
stunned by all of this coming and going,
this silence, this laughter, these tears,
your heart's hieroglyphics still unspoken.

In This Late Night Silence

In this late-night silence, no one here but me,
I am being slowly deprogrammed,
unraveled, unhinged, unfurled.
In this ever-widening space of no time,
there is nothing to say,
my song, unwritten,
now being hummed in another world,
a thousand Zen koans
spinning in great circles around me –
the one who waits for an answer
out for a stroll and noticing
a single daisy.

You Are the Water

The words I speak
to tell the world
about your unspeakable magnificence
are barely visible holes
at the bottom of a bucket
I raise from an ancient well.
You are the water
and the feeling that comes
from quenching my thirst.

My True Profession

I finally understand what my true profession is –
I'm a stripper,
I strip away everything unnecessary,
whatever separates me from myself
and you.
My efforts, no matter how heroic I think they are,
don't really matter all that much,
whatever I forget to strip away is stripped away for me.
Any way you look at it, I'm a stripper,
totally naked on a good day
and still not sure where all the money goes.

Letting It All Down

There are women in the world with long hair
who like to put it up, twirl it and stack it and swirl it
high on top of their heads, clamped and clipped,
held, sometimes, in place, with long sticks or pins
or multi-colored bands that come five to a pack,
or maybe, on a Sunday afternoon, just a simple red scarf.

It takes many shapes, their hair,
a bun tightly wound and worn just before a formal affair,
perhaps a concert in the drawing room
or, on a more casual day,
a kind of waterfall splashing just for fun,
strands of silky hair going this way and that.

The reasons, if you can call them that, are many,
perhaps it is a summer day
and the back of their neck is way too hot
or maybe it's simply time for a new look,
a subtle shift of personality,
here in this world where time is passing.

I really don't have a clue,
and yet, without a doubt, there is a moment
amidst all of the changes in this grand opera of life
when the woman lets down her hair,
letting it fall to the place it can fall no further from,
nothing propping it up, nothing holding it in place,
no style except the one she was born with,
wind playing with each strand
or, if the air just happens to be still (as we all long to be),
simply laying there, at rest, done with everything,
nothing on her list.

Cruising with Rumi

On a bone cold February afternoon,
23 miles from home in a rented Toyota,
I listen to Rumi 800 years gone
from praising everything that breathed,
my heart racing with him through towns with no name.

Lights are flashing everywhere, especially behind me,
not white like those that lit up Rumi's eyes, no,
more like red, the kind that signal stop and oops
and maybe I should slow down and pull over.

Rumi, on the 5-CD changer, is unconcerned,
his monologue of love, making perfect sense
as I witness a large man of the law approaching
and reach for my license,
not the poetic kind,
the one no one shows their mother,
but the *other* one with the bad photo
even as the uniformed man now standing tall by my door
beckons me to roll down my window
and announces, like a small-town accountant
wishing he was home for lunch with his wife,
my speed,
which, he informs me, was 20 over the limit,
Rumi still holding forth beneath an ancient Persian moon.

He has kind eyes,
my sudden companion for the moment in his well-pressed
uniform,
kind eyes and a smile that speaks of long winters
keeping roads safe for travelers like me
who, somehow, much have missed the sign
about a mile back,
veiled as it was by that old willow tree
and the last few rays of light
finding their way past the steepest hill in town,
the one where all the kids go sledding,
kids, as far as I can tell,
who have never heard of Rumi,
the officer of the law
or me.

Slightly Out of Frame

Sitting in the garden beneath a pale blue sky,
she pointed her camera at me and paused
as if I was the only man in the world,
then she clicked, smiled and showed me what she saw:
Bougainvilleas,
flaming pink bougainvilleas –
many of them,
me just slightly out of frame.

Longing Wells Up from Within

I am waiting for you beneath a hot sun
in the middle of nowhere,
you have not yet arrived,
nor do I have the faintest clue
when you will appear.
Half of the time my eyes are open,
the other half, they are closed.
It really doesn't matter,
your absence is the biggest illusion,
filling me, as it does,
with more presence
than anyone else's arrival.

The Beautiful Sadness of Longing

There is a beautiful kind of sadness –
one most people think they shouldn't feel
that needs to be celebrated,
or, if not celebrated, then at least welcomed
like the evening's last beggar at your door.

This sadness is divine,
the experience of what most people consider to be an absence,
but, in reality,
is the presence of the divine longing for the Beloved.

It would be easy to conclude
that this feeling is a disconnection from joy,
an unfortunate amnesia
that would make an easy target
for well-meaning givers of advice
to quote from their favorite scripture,
but I am not talking about this garden variety of sadness,
I am talking about another kind –
a holy melancholy that sculpts, deepens, and refines from within.

Like the dusk that follows day, it is not devoid of light –
only another shade of light,
yes, it is darker, but so what?
Isn't it the darkness that allows the stars to shine?

When a human being is in the presence of their Beloved,
it is easy to feel joy.
Like leaving home in the middle of a storm,
it is easy to get wet there.
but when the Beloved departs
(ah, the paradox, the late night debates –
does the Beloved ever depart?),
an uncomfortable feeling arises,
the moon is full, but you are empty –
thirsty for something to fill you again,
the only thing to drink a bucket of tears
and you cannot find the handle.

Off in the distance you hear the sound of a cello.
Is it sad or beautiful?

Drawn by the music, you follow, feeling your way,
singing silent songs of praise
and wondering if what you hear
is the sound of your own voice or your name being called.

You know and have always known,
that the Beloved has left the world behind as a gift,
but you do not want the gift,
you want the Giver.

The Slightly Overweight Museum Security Guard

He stands there barely,
a kind of slow-moving piece of performance art
just a bit off stage,
not understanding
the apparently fabulous shapes
in the next room
recently described in the New York Times,
though he is, indeed, dressed for the part.

His hands, lightly clenched behind his back,
hold no brushes, no paint, no cloth,
his eyes, unsure of much
here in this large white room,
stare off into somebody else's distance
while the rest of him,
curious for the moment,
wonders if the tuna fish sandwich
his wife packed for lunch today,
will be quite enough.

Now he is leaning up against the wall,
now he is not,
now he is not leaning up against the wall,
now he is.

When I Grow Up

When I grow up, I want to be nobody,
do nothing, go nowhere,
having already arrived a long time ago.
When I listen to my voice mail,
no one will be talking,
no one asking me for anything at all,
my need to hear a voice, other than yours,
completely gone,
me being done with proving or improving myself,
done with what's next and any more stories to tell,
this so-called "me," like a single drop of water
dissolved into the fabulous sea of life,
nothing left to say,
each breath a prayer needing no answer.

Perhaps I will make a paper airplane out of my to-do list,
fly it out the window and watch it flutter in the wind,
perhaps, when a nearby child picks it up,
forgetting everything and everyone else,
I will hear birds singing as if for the first time.

Written During an Unexpected Jazz Concert

The hieroglyphic message of this moment
can never be explained,
but I can tell you what it *feels* like.

It feels like walking into a room
where the most beautiful woman in the world
is slowly undressing and, in her own sweet time,
glances over her shoulder in my direction,
me unsure
of whether or not she is looking at me
or seeing something else in the distance.

A blue jay?
The moon?
Her reflection in the mirror?

There is absolutely no density here,
no plan, no ground –
just the perfume of a perfect moment beyond time –
the place where Rumi dwells
and Mozart,
the space between molecules,
the pause between breath,
the realm where all of us exist
when there is nowhere else to go.

Freedom, my friends, freedom,
somersaulting into infinity without going anywhere,
kind of like Chuck Berry walking into a guitar store
before he knew what music was.

Find Yourself, Lose Yourself

If you want to find God, find yourself,
if you want to find yourself, lose yourself,
if you want to lose yourself, be found
by that which is beyond finding and losing.
In the meantime, be happy, be kind!
Be grateful for the gift of life.

THREE

"We all know that there is a drop in the ocean,
but very few know there is an ocean in the drop."

– Kabir

The Falcon and the Falconer

I am the falcon,
you are the falconer,
always I am coming back to you,
my soaring skyward just a strategy
to gather speed for my ultimate return.
How you have trained me is a mystery –
the way you've tamed my restless heart,
it is not with fear, I do not fear you,
it is not with food,
there is prey enough for me everywhere I fly,
more it is the way you offer me your arm,
a place to land, a second skin,
scented with the wild musk of one who waits for me,
what I would be if I would be a man.

It is a wonderful game the two of us play –
this coming and going, this circular ballet.
Each time you loosen the loops around my legs
and signal me to fly, I remember
what it is to rise for the first time,
it is here I find my rest, my home.

Untethered, still I do not move,
needing only to be close to you, my Falconer.
It is this that beats my wings, releases me to sky,
rides the unseen currents of the air
and though I notice other things:
the tops of trees, a cloud, a nimble rabbit on the ground,
all I see is you, holding out your arm to me,
even as a thousand other falcons overhead,
each within your view, circle closer,
spiral down, descend,
yet still I know that I am next
and this is the perfect moment of my own return.

The World Is a Milkweed Pod

If you knew how much you already had,
you wouldn't waste a single second
wanting anything else,
the entire universe is yours
and still you think you need something else.
The world, my friend, is a milkweed pod,
the more you try to grab it,
the more it floats away.

Pause, breathe, and extend your hand slowly,
receive what's always been yours,
the legal work's been done a million years ago,
throw a party,
invite your friends and all your neighbors, too,
greet them, feed them, love them,
give them something cool to drink,
dance until you cannot stand.

No Portal, No Gate

There is a place between day and night,
between now and later,
between body and soul.
There is no entrance to this place,
no portal, no gate.
You cannot get there by going,
only by already being there.
It is, this place,
a secret chamber of the heart,
but only for those who can keep a secret.
You have no proof it exists and never will,
the more you look for it, the less you will see,
the more you listen for it, the less you will hear,
this mystery cannot be attained, only received,
a bestowal it is, a gift,
like the first few drops of dew
on this morning's spider web.

Speechless

It's not what I say,
it's what I don't say,
but every time I say nothing,
what I do not say
leaves so much to be said,
I am speechless,
maybe that's why
Groucho raised his eyebrows
and Jesus raised the dead.

The Fling

Last night
I printed all my poems,
put them in a plastic bag
and crawled out my bedroom window
to the roof.
There I stood beneath the moon,
grabbed everything I could,
and flung 40 years of words to the sky.
Many white pages,
like plucked wings of a mythical bird,
flapped and fluttered to the ground,
the first complaint,
I imagine,
of the man who comes
to mow the lawn tomorrow morning.

Keep This Window Open

Is an open window missing anything –
a pane of glass, a curtain,
a sheet of plywood in case a hurricane comes?
Breezes enter through this window
or should I say where a window was,
there being nothing now but empty space,
no way to separate
the inside from the outside,
where I'm standing now
from where I will be standing later,
you from me.

Who I am *is* this empty space,
this portal to everything,
before a single need arises or regret.

Keep this window open wide, my friend,
even in a storm,
while the floor may get wet
and it will seem as if, sometimes, you are all alone,
the tears you shed will dry everything,
the silence now filled
with the holy thunder of yourself.

The Impulse To Listen

Beethoven, the first time he realized he was deaf,
still listened,
what he heard was far beyond sound,
more like the place where sound originates.
You can call it music if you like,
but the real symphony is playing
inside the impulse to listen
even when there is nothing to hear
and no one on stage
to applaud for.

A Child Upon Waking

My heart opens like my eyes,
involuntarily,
a child upon waking,
amazed
without a single plan for the day,
and though it blinks,
still it sees,
and though it cannot speak,
it beats,
a late-night drummer
alone in his room,
the entire universe his gig.

A Single Drop of Water on a Spider Web

There is a moment and that moment is now,
a single drop of water on a spider web,
a warrior sharpening his sword,
your child, whose first word
is just about to be pronounced –
the moment when everything stops
and nothing needs to begin again,
your first kiss,
a beggar's smile, rain,
and the glorious moment when you let it all go –
all that trying,
all those promises made too late.

What remains?

Everything and nothing, the place where the path begins –
your next breath the only proof you need that God exists.

Written in the Parking Lot of My Health Club

I am a rosebush, newly pruned,
my flowers trimmed for the long haul,
the core of myself less visible than ever,
but bursting with life.
There is a season for everything, I guess,
even songbirds sleep,
and lovers, spent for the night, stare into space.
Is it the sun now rising in my breath?
The moon?
Alone in the cave of my heart, but not at all lonely,
I feel the flaming bud of creation opening in my cells.

What is happening?

I am sitting in the parking lot of my health club,
gym clothes on the seat beside me,
overwhelmed by poetry.
This is crazy!
I came here to move my body,
but it is my soul, instead, getting the workout
sitting here in the front seat of my Subaru,
storm clouds above me, James Taylor on the radio,
"Goodnight moonlight ladies,
Rockabye Sweet Baby James,"
tears now rising like a thousand suns inside me.

There is an oyster in the shell,
a song in my heart, a heaven in the hell,
a union when we part, a birth inside the death,
a kiss inside the moon and God within my breath.
Such is the great mystery of life,
such is the game we play,
everything we want we have
and everything we have will one day fade away.

Ah, the great paradox!
The one you seek is seeking you,
the one you praise is praising, too.
The object of your devotion
is not an object at all, but a vibration
having taken human form,
the face of infinity, the mask of creation,
the ultimate mirror into which you look
and, upon seeing your reflection, dance,
even if you choose not to move at all.

Equanimity

Can you throw away
the roses
with the same love
you proclaimed
upon giving them
to your Beloved
when they were
in full bloom?

Just This Crazy Laughter

Now that you have shown me who I am,
what do you want me to do?
Sing your praises?
No can do, I'm mute.
Write love songs?
Ha!
My hands are shaking and so is the ground.
Oh, my Friend,
an ocean of fools I have become,
a lunatic walking on moonlight.

This is not at all what I imagined when first we met,
not even close,
even if my story could be told,
no one would believe me,
I have no proof,
not a single shred of evidence,
just this crazy laughter
and the kind of late-night sighing
that comes when there is nothing left to say.

I Used To Write Love Poems

I used to write love poems,
now I collect them
like small shells on the beach
only the locals know about,
there is nothing inside them,
they are empty,
but when you put your ear to the opening
and really listen,
you can hear the ocean.

Disguised as Myself

Disguised as myself,
nowhere to go,
I look into the mirror
of your perfect radiance
and there, disappear
once again,
the mask I am gone,
the long journey done,
breath, the lover
I've been looking for
all these many years.

A Great Sadness Is Upon Me

One

A great sadness is upon me,
like a mist in a forest no one can see,
it does not lift, this mist,
even when butterflies find their way through it
and wolves.
Not yet a wise man, still I know
what people will say when I confess to them this feeling of mine.
"Get a hobby,"
"Count your blessings,"
"Look at the bright side of life."
Spare me, please,
I am not looking for answers, my friends,
nor am I looking for questions.
I am just sitting here,
an unopened love letter on a Thursday afternoon,
a great sadness upon me.

Two

I have made the only decision worth making today –
stop trying so hard,
the glorious gifts of God cannot be gotten that way,
they can only be received
like rain to the thirsty,
like a long embrace unrequested,

like the way a baby looks at a stranger
and the stranger no longer feels strange.
Discipline is not the path to the heart
being a disciple is.
Of *what*, you ask?
Of that which exists everywhere, all the time, and forever,
needing nothing but itself to shine,
radiant, self-effulgent, alive.
It has no name, this mirror of light,
even if you give it one, like a lover,
in a fit of adoration, needing an object of devotion.

Three

Here's what I know:
Nothing.
Here's what I've accomplished so far:
less than that,
there's a sky overhead
and ground beneath my feet,
everything else
is simply way too much to think about.

Four

One of the illusions of life
is that something needs to be done,
a field to mow,
a room to clean,
a destination to reach.
Actually, it's the opposite,
something needs to be undone,
untangled, unraveled, unmade,
like the spider web I weave each morning
pearled with dew,
to catch what I already have.

Five

On my death bed,
where I will not make love,
it is very likely,
after my long slow ascent
into whatever comes next,
that I will find myself
apologizing to all the people
I was never quite able to love enough,
wishing I had been a much bigger field
for them to dance in,
dance and sing and laugh or do nothing at all
if that's what they wanted.
Like you, for example.

Six

I have come to the end of the line.
This one!
The one above,
the one with only two words:
This –
as in what exists right now,
and *one* –
that which is irreducible,
what was there in the beginning,
though I realize, of course,
it is possible that something existed before it,
something pristine, holy, and divine,
but please don't call it zero,
really, don't, I beg you,
your cleverness only reminds me of mine.
Before *that*, too.

Seven

I am a guest in my own house,
I am not the owner
even if you think I am.
I am just passing through,
like a breeze through a half-opened window
like a thought in your mind,
like a piece of thread through the eye of a needle,
tailor nowhere in sight.

Just a Little Bit Longer

I am sitting here now,
looking out a window,
writing this poem,
the fewest words I know
to say what cannot be said.
I want to give this poem away,
I do,
but it will not leave me,
now a kind of perfume in the air
lingering like a lover who does not want to go.
Shall I give this poem to you, my friend?
Will you accept it?
Will you hold it to your breast?
And if you do, here is my request:
gaze at something today
just a little bit longer than you normally would.

Where My Life Begins

The space between thoughts
is where my life begins,
God's temple, cathedral and mosque,
no incense needs to be lit there,
the perfect perfume of God's air
present.
No prayers need to be spoken,
the pause between now and
whatever comes next,
the perfect invocation.

The Ecstatic Wound of Longing

You are the only one who has never deceived me,
the only one who received my fear without shame,
looked to no one else when I called for help,
saw my real face behind the mask of disillusionment,
free of needing me, you healed the lover within,
sick from years of being chilled by this world,
you were the only one to enjoy me,
to adore and restore me even when I
crawled like a bug to find my own bed in the darkness,
you were the one to sing to me
long before ordinary birds called to each other at sunrise,
sent me fragrance of rose through my half-opened window,
opened the ecstatic wound of longing
stuck inside the fury of this ultimate need for you.

Broom

The kitchen is dirty,
there is dust between the floorboards,
the harder I sweep
the more bristles break off,
dust flies and settles again,
coughing,
I have swept up the broom.

Waking Up Today

This morning when I woke up,
no alarm clock, no birds, no appointments,
I noticed there was a marching band inside my head,
many costumed characters wanting to make some noise,
express themselves,
play whatever it was they held in their two hands.
They were already moving,
these horn-carrying players of something or other,
going somewhere,
purposeful on their way up the street
and I had just awakened,
feet not even on the ground.
Was I late for something? Did I need to catch up?
Or was there another song to play,
the one with no notes, no strutting, no sound?
That's when I sat up,
put my feet on the floor
and took another breath.
I breathed. That's all I did.
I breathed, nothing else,
an orchestra of love poised inside me,
glad for the pause,
conductor nowhere in sight,
baton in hand, smiling.

FOUR

"Security is mostly a superstition.
Life is either a daring adventure or nothing."
– Helen Keller

The Difference Between a Grocery List and a Poem

Poetry is
really nothing more
than a well-formed list
of unexpected words and images,
one line following another,
like this one, for example,
and this one,
each adding
a little something extra
to the flow,
a shade of meaning,
a wink, a hint of perfume,
not unlike what follows,
perhaps something you have carried
in your pocket for weeks without even knowing it,
crumpled:
Bananas (one bunch),
tomatoes (ripe),
three avocados,
hummus, pickles, feta cheese,
a pint of chocolate ice cream.

Tell me, what is the difference between
a grocery list and a poem?
Give up? Good!

A grocery list gives you things to get,
a poem gets you things to give,
things you will not find in Aisle 3,
but high up in the many selves you are,
especially the one
who likes to count how long it will take
to get from your car in the parking lot
to the front door of the supermarket
by how many haikus she can recite.

The One for Whom It All Makes Sense

I have written a thousand poems for you
that have never left my room,
they fill the pages of notebooks
stacked high on a shelf
no one can reach,
orphans they are, beggars
afraid they are not noble enough for the King,
would never make it past his guards.
I make a vain attempt
to dress them up,
disguise their ridiculous origins,
but still they smell bad.
Even so, there are times, late at night,
when the world has shut down and they think I'm asleep,
I can almost hear them talking to each other,
conjuring ways to make it to your court.
Oh, the arguments they have! The brawls!
The lunatic moments of staking their ground.
Some of them actually believe
that all they need is a shower and a shave,
others, unsure of who they are
or might have been,
insist on practicing, all night long,
their perfect way of greeting you.

Of course, there is much to be said
for these backroom bards,
these arm-wrestling vagrants from another world.
Indeed, if I was dead,
my slightly deaf biographer, after paying his due respects
to my dear, sweet wife,
would borrow them just long enough
to search for pearls, find the perfect turn of phrase,
the sudden storm of brilliance
even my harshest critics would have to praise.
He'd think of clever little titles for the tome,
describing, in his mournfully halting way,
the "man who left his muse too soon"
or some such thing
that might make you wonder
why I never gave these poems to you –
the one for whom it all makes sense
even when it doesn't.

Almost a Definition of Poetry

Poetry:
frost on the window
just before it snows,
looking through it
changes everything you see.

I Rode My Breath

I rode my breath to the penthouse,
but there was no one there,
just a roof garden open to the sky
and the full moon overhead.

Found in Old Journals after 40 Years

Two years ago, I sold my home after 26 years of living there with my wife and two children. In the process of emptying out the house, I found 60 journals I'd been carrying around for the past 40 years. What follows are selected excerpts in no particular order.

Words are only burrs on the path
through the high-country brush with God.

I sit in the cave of myself,
alone with my breath,
there is nobody else here but me
in this cool, dark hollow of my soul.

Night falls around me
like the arms of a lover
widowed by daylight
and seeking the warmth of another.

The one who yearns for God must die
like flowers to the fruit,
must fall to the root
around the tree of life that gives us all shade.

He walks on water, I walk on ice,
but when I lay my head at his feet
I remember there is nowhere to go.
Here. Only here. Always here.

There are angels buried in my flesh.

How deep can I look into someone's eyes?
Only to the place where they are looking for you,
unafraid of what they'll find.

I must be in love or is it insane?

Who can receive me?
Who is deep enough for me to disappear into?

He joins heaven and hell
with a wave of his hand,
his breath, the wand,
his smile the ground I walk upon.

Void of all tears, sworn to silence,
I lose everything, once again, but myself.

Suture the ragged wound closed,
let all your scars be roads to follow home.

I take photographs with words,
the resolution of a thousand lifetimes
waiting for you.

Like a breeze through lace curtains,
enter softly and stay with me a while.

I bend because he has removed the weight.

She wanted more space. I gave her the universe.

I am melting,
I am burning at both ends,
and what I see by this flickering light,
is more than enough.

Oh Master of my soul,
you have ignited the brittle tinder of my heart.

The closer I get to you,
the more I see how far away I am.

Who else listens to me when, speechless,
my heart begins to sing? Who?

I have gone to meet you in your secret place,
but when I arrived, neither of us were there.

Forget about ashes on your forehead,
let your whole body be consumed in flames.

My pen, today, is a butterfly net,
The sky is full of wings.

The only lines I want to wait on
are the ones around your eyes.

Who can this Master be,
the one whose path is strewn with rose petals?

When You Walk into a Room

When you walk into the room,
all the poets feel a sudden urge to praise,
dancers want to move,
singers ache to raise their voices high
for all those times
they foolishly chose silence instead.

This impulse to express,
this surging forward into form,
is absolutely involuntary, tidal, primal, pure.

The poet's fingers twitch,
the dancer moves inside her shoes,
the singer breathes,
already receiving roses
from the grateful choreographer of her heart.

Give Everything You Have

Give everything you have,
and after you have given,
give what's left,
after you give what's left,
give what remains,
after giving that,
give the feeling of having given,
after giving the feeling
of having given,
give what you get
for having given,
then give again,
never stopping, always giving,
and should it come to pass that you forget,
forgive yourself immediately,
then begin again,
giving everything you have,
and after you have given,
give what's left.

Centrifugal

I want to get centrifugal with you,
spin to the edges
of the outermost orbit of who you are
and there open a small cafe with no name,
muffins rising, 24/7,
the most comfortable chair in the room
always empty for whoever enters next.
Music is the language there.
Whenever something needs to be said
the person closest to the piano
plays.

Having Arrived by Already Being There

Desire is wanting what you don't have,
longing is wanting what you do,
but if you knew how much you already had,
you would have it all,
so much so, that a million lifetimes
would not be enough to give it all away.

Here's as simple as it gets:
there is an underground spring within us all,
the water of life that quenches all thirst
and all we need to do is drink.

Yes, the world is beautiful,
but only if you are,
otherwise, it is just the centrifugal pull
of wandering away from yourself,
the merry-go-round ring always out of reach,
the thought of love, but not the love itself.

You can marvel at the stars all you want,
you can praise a single blade of grass,
but it is only because your eyes are open
that any of this matters.

Yes, God's nature is a gift –
the earth, the bee, the butterfly –
but it is only human nature that allows us to open it,
the impulse to see beyond the wrapping
and be seized,
pirates on our own ship of this moment's sailing.

Here Is the Secret

Here is the secret:
there is no secret,
but if that's the secret,
then there *is* a secret,
and if there is a secret,
then the second line of this stanza
is a complete and utter lie
even though I was doing my best
to speak the truth.

Seek the One Beyond the Veil

I have waited for him, too, my friend,
sat by the window of my self
with only the light in these dark eyes to see,
gazed into grey skies of late afternoons
without a sign of his approach, companionless.
Walking led nowhere, nor did sitting still.

We must abide in this nether world, you say,
to test our faith, our trust, our love?
Not so, say, I. Not so.

Seek the one beyond the veil and he will come,
touch you without hands,
speak to you with silence,
plant you in the fertile soil of your soul
so you might one day flower and bear fruit.

Do not be satisfied with the promise of his coming,
he is here and I have seen him dance.

My Poems are Like a Persian Rug

My poems are like a Persian rug,
in each there is a flaw,
a word, a phrase, a rhythm off,
an over-reaching metaphor.
So close they are to what I feel,
but close is all they are,
like wooden spokes are to the wheel,
like children wishing on a star.

The Slow Moving into Empty Space

What is it you are trying to find
that will make you happy enough to stop seeking?
Is it someone to hold you,
or something so pure you would have no need to be held?
Is not your ceaseless wandering a sign of your arrival,
your willingness to trust that which
moves you beyond stillness?
Is not your drifting
really just an orbit you will never understand?

Where you see vagrancy, my friend,
I see slow ancestral dancing,
shadows on rock reaching skyward
great, great grandfathers and mothers before them
patient for a rhythm and a song.
Is not this slow moving into empty space
what a human being does –
this apparent aimlessness
merely the divine geometry of own reconvergence?

Wake up, my friend!
It doesn't matter what you do or how you refuse
the sweet urgency of breath,
your holy migration will never end,
even the dead decompose,
become soil for the rose they gladly
would have given their Beloved
if only they had stopped trying so hard to understand
why they were so restless,
so easily moved.

Plum Tree

Today, I imagined everything I owned
had reduced itself
down to a singular plum tree –
the kind an 85-year-old Japanese poet,
sipping sake,
likes to tend at the end of the day.
This plum tree,
this solitary plum tree,
had suddenly become the still, ripe center of my life –
the axis around which all my desires dissolve,
stunned as I am,
purple fruit everywhere.

The Seed Once Sown, The Rune

I talk too much, too loud, too soon,
like one who pulls a sword from stone
and speaks before the King has had his turn.
My words are ghosts of moments gone,
the poetry you want to hear is not my own,
but yours, the sacred sound long buried in your bones –
the seed once sown, the rune,
something born within you to be told.

This is what you want to hear,
the perfect eloquence of one upon the throne,
whose prayer, these words, are heard
before a single word is said.
Live there! Breathe deep! Fly!
Free yourself and if the angels die,
know you'll be dancing in the air.
That's the poetry you want to hear!

What you really want is this:
the lyrical flood of fullness within,
the drowning in bliss,
the letting down, like mother's milk,
of all there ever is –
the place where all the poets you have ever loved
are riding homeward on a train, alone,
looking out a window on a perfect summer day.
What they see is only their reflection
and just beyond it all, golden fields of hay.
Somewhere in between them both their breathing slows,
they close their eyes and pause,
clear they never have to write again or think.

This is the poetry you long to hear,
when all the poets turn for home
and all their blood has turned to ink.

Now You See It

We are here for just a little while,
freshly fallen snow
on a half-opened rose.
That's it. No more.
It doesn't take much
for the vanishing act to begin,
a burst of sun,
a sudden breeze,
someone knocking on your door
and you are gone,
done,
a tale told by a friend
tending her garden at dusk.

The Only Question Left for Me Tonight

The only question left for me tonight is this:
do I write by candlelight or moonlight?

Both have their advantages, you see:
candlelight, softening everything around it,
evokes lifetimes of lovers,
none of whom ever want to take their leave,
only breathe into each other,
luxuriating in the moment,
silence the manger they now find themselves in,
fused breath rising
like a sun inside the same shared horizon.

Ah... yes... candlelight...
a mighty fine contender it is, the poet's muse,
and I haven't even yet gotten to the moon yet –
lighting the way to monastery walls
and all those haiku years tending plum trees
in a garden swept by monks
so they might finally catch a glimpse of their Master,
the one for whom they traveled such great distances to see.

Ah... such liquid sweetness there is in this grand elixir of life
where only love exists, my friends, only love,
love and the second question of this poem:

"Who is it that moves my hand just so?"

A weed in the wind it is,
bed sheets being shaken out on a far hillside,
God's mime holding his pen as if it was a 17th century sword,
its handle so heavy only a light heart could lift it tonight.

Homeless

Homeless,
with just a few stars to guide me,
I am a bum in a roadside temple,
cheater
whose deck of cards
has long since been stolen.

Golden Nomad of Ecstasy

Alone beneath a full moon once again,
I gather together all I can give,
milkweed, tears, a bouquet of cold fingers
and the awful silence between too many promises.

Everything else is a dream,
a glove dropped and awaiting your warm hand.
Won't you break this bubble of unknowing?
Won't you end this masquerade?

If you don't come and claim me, Lord,
from this fantasy of loving you
what in the world will happen to me?
Will I wander forever in this unwritten scripture
like some parable of faithfulness,
seeing you in others' eyes, but never in your own?
Will I live? Will I die?
Should I ride the undertow inside me
back to the shell of our first meeting?

My heart was a desert then, my body a stone,
but you, golden nomad of ecstasy,
you burned the world away in a glance,
spoke to me like thunder,
turned my endless wandering into pure dance.

Today, slightly confused and needing a mother,
I find myself leaping –
not in search of you, no,
because of you.

Every Drop of Water Is a Jewel

We are all asleep, dreaming we're awake,
we dream of waking,
then share our dream with others who are also sleeping.
Deep inside their dream, they comment on ours,
meanwhile, the entire universe is flying through space
and every drop of water is a jewel.

What will you be thinking of on your death bed?
What will you wish you had really experienced?

FIVE

"And the day came when the risk to remain tight in a bud was more painful than the risk it took to blossom."

– Anais Nin

Written in Newark Airport, Gate C71

I reach out to you,
but who is reaching and why?
What is this mad attraction I suddenly feel,
the iron filing I am now magnetized by you?

Resistance is the only sin I know,
like a flower refusing to bloom,
like a lover afraid to love.

This moving towards you
has nothing to do with my completion,
I am already complete,
it has nothing to do with God,
(you showed me that a long time ago).

It is simpler than that,
way simpler,
more like two children splashing around
in a very large puddle,
neither needing to get back home
or change their clothes.

Lunatic

I live in a sky with no clouds,
no color, no sun,
neither can I tell
if it is a leaf or butterfly
that floats to the earth below.
Though the coming storm brings rain
and tides of blood within me
there's no one close enough to hear –
only a full moon overhead
and a few lunatics walking on moonlight,
singing, singing.

There is a Fabulous Underground Club

There is a fabulous underground club not far from you
where all the ecstatic musicians since the beginning of time
are playing, eyes on fire.
They speak a thousand different languages,
but understand each other completely,
having endured long winters, several times a day,
with no one near enough to listen or bring them tea.

None of this matters now.

Here in this cave of pure delight,
calling on muses spinning in great circles,
they are free, holding a high note together,
in perfect harmony,
like the hand of God.

Come to the End of the Shore

If you want to worship God today
come to the end of the shore and sing,
leave your friends behind for the moment,
your book, your hat, your shoes,
give up waiting for the sun.

Cleaning Up

This morning I had a huge realization.
Actually, it was more like a revelation –
some kind of holy cocktail paradigm shift,
breakthrough, aha, and epiphany all rolled into one.

Then, again, I might be exaggerating in a lame attempt to
capture your attention and say what I really wanted to say.

And here it is:

I am spending entirely way too much time writing.
How do I know?
Because there are dust balls in just about
every corner of my apartment,
dishes in the sink
and many piles of paper stacked in various places
with cryptic notes to myself on top of them –
stuff like: "Deal with this now!"

While my poetry may be approximating pristine,
my kitchen is not,
nor is my living room, office, or bathroom.

I'm sure if Charles Bukowski dropped by,
everything would be totally fine.
Maybe the two of us would knock back a few tequilas
next to the pile of dishes and curse a lot,
but it's Buddha I'm more concerned about
and the extraordinary Prem Rawat.

How would I feel if either one them walked in unannounced?

Of course, I could give each of them the manuscript of my
soon-to-be published book
in a clever attempt to distract them while I tidied up,
but I have a strong suspicion they would see right through me
like they always do,
which is why, this morning,
I spent the first day of the New Year cleaning up.

My sink is sparkling clean,
even the faucets shine.

If the Dalai Lama wants to use my bathroom, I'm ready.
The dust balls are gone,
in their place, clean corners.
My bed is made,
my clothes, just back from the laundromat,
are folded and put away.

My New Year's resolution?

That anyone, anytime can walk into my home
and feel just as good as if they had walked into one of my poems
or even my mind.

The flowers will be fresh,
the kitchen will be swept
and there will be absolutely no difference
between what I write and how I live.

Or, I could just hire a housekeeper.

Rumi on the Front Porch

First, I removed all the clocks from my house,
then I removed the mirrors.
I watered the plants, trimmed the dead leaves
and swept the kitchen,
then I went outside and sat on the front porch,
Rumi book in hand.

I just sat there, doing nothing.
A few people walked by,
I waved at them and they waved back,
a dog barked,
I thought of a few things I had thought of before,
then I opened the book.

Jalal ad-Din Muhammad Rumi lived 800 years ago,
but he was rocking right next to me on my front porch today.
He said something funny that made us both laugh
and, for a moment, we totally forgot who we were.
Then Rumi started singing a song that made no sense,
no sense whatsoever –
kind of like a flock of drunken birds,
flying in a strange pattern,
with the wind at their backs.

What I Have Understood

What I have understood a baby already knows,
so do lunatics, lovers, and monks.
We are all born radiant, holy and divine,
Buddhas of the great beyond,
then, slowly, with almost no warning,
we enter the Great Amnesia,
a lifetime spent looking for a key we never lost
to open a lock that was never closed
to open a door that does not exist.
Wardens to ourselves, we rattle our cage,
complain about the food
and count the days until we are free,
while in the very next room –
a flamenco dancer poised at the entrance –
the most outrageous party in the world is going on,
everyone laughing and singing
and rising as they move across the floor
like endless bubbles from a newly opened bottle of champagne.

When I Was a Young Man

When I was a young man,
I thought God could be found by looking,
or, in my case, staring.
The harder I looked, I reasoned,
the faster I would find.

Only later did I realize
that what I was looking for was looking for me,
that all I had to do was stop trying so hard.

Love is not something to get.
Love is something you are.

Be Empty Like the Sky

Be empty
like the sky,
the only cloud
on the horizon
smoke from a fire
you started
to warm a total stranger
when the sun went down.

Am I Breathing or Am I Being Breathed?

Am I breathing or am I being breathed?
Who is doing what to whom?
This "me" and "mine"
are apparently just holograms.

Dust that speaks is what I have become,
you across the room with broom in hand
and a smile wider than the universe.

Wait!
There's a pile of words over there in the corner,
a verb, an adjective, a noun.
Someone coughs and clears their throat,
a sound now prelude to something needing to be said,
Moses just back from the desert,
the man from Nazareth just about to wake the dead.

Outside, birds are singing,
the moon just a sliver,
my heart completely full.

The Swing

There is a swing
in the sky of your self
that has been there forever,
maybe longer.
What it's attached to
is anybody's guess,
any many people do.
What's more important
is whether or not
you are going to grab on
and go for the ride.

Get Wet

People ask me
what it was like being with you
five days in a row
in the middle of nowhere.
Here's what I tell them:
It was like spinning around in a monsoon,
cup in hand, trying to catch the rain.
Every time I noticed that my cup was full,
I opened my mouth to sing,
but my mouth filled up with water.
I gulped, I drank, I bailed my boat of joy.
Somehow, in between the tidal waves of love
and my odd little habit of trying to figure out
what in the world was going on,
I heard what you said:
"Get wet! Get wet!"

What Moves Us All to Dream

What moves us all to dream,
to think, to love, to act,
to give it up for some great cause
or double back to pause before our plans
of having more or getting there
or going to the country fair
is the same for everyone –
the sage, the fool, the king.
the self-appointed ministers of fun

Albert Einstein said it best
or maybe it was Rumi
both of whom were missing links
from this to that, from here to there,
mystics of the unseen arts,
demystifying what it is that moves the air
and the human heart.

Still I wonder what it is I thirst for in my bones
and what will be enough to feel.
Is it what I see with these two eyes
or what I know beyond them both
is always just a bit concealed –
that which seizes me from deep within,
the mirror of my soul,
my other half, my perfect twin,
the one who knows but doesn't tell
or if he does, it's just enough
to dig my tunnel deeper to the well
where all the seekers that I am have come to drink
long before the first parable was told.

Like an Old Mexican Woman

These days I write poetry
like an old Mexican woman
crocheting a red hat for her neighbor's son.
At her feet a dog is sleeping,
moving every five minutes or so
to keep the flies away.

Does Anyone Understand the Work of a Master?

Does anyone understand the work of a Master?
I don't think so.
Even those who weep for joy
are only looking through a pinhole,
a crack in time and space,
tourists peeking through a fence.

Dazed by the light that finds its way through,
they are more like dancers than knowers,
spinning around the maypole of an unexpected ecstasy,
their sudden expressions of love,
over which they have no control,
now witnessed by a few locals
out for a stroll and a smoke
and wondering, as they are,
why these strange people are laughing for no reason,
hearts on fire,
their unspoken words, like painted rocks,
plummeting to the bottom of a very still pond
on a night no one wants to end.

Radiant Being of Light

Radiant being of light,
vortex of love,
alchemist supreme,
magnifier of prayer,
the one I dream about
and the one who wakes me from the dream,
why the dervish spins
and the earth,
teacher, teaching, and the taught,
first breath, last breath,
what lovers look for in each other,
but rarely find,
center around which everything revolves,
endless night of love
and the ecstatic aching of a moon-howling heart
that does not want the morning to come.

The One Who Teaches from Within

I want to tell you about my Master,
the one who teaches from within,
that like a heartbeat longing to be heard
becomes the twin I never knew I had,
Him! That one!
He is calling me,
not with music, that would be too easy,
but with longing – that's his choir!

I cannot describe this man,
my words only exclude,
limit by defining.
Better simply to say, "the one I love,"
answer to a prayer much too subtle
for anyone else to hear.
Him! That One! Keeper of the flame,
who I am, was, and will be
when there's no one around to remember my name,
why you like candlelight,
want a child, dream –
the one with no other master plan but love.

I have met this man, or should I say, observed,
struck dumb by his simplicity
and the unspeakable glory of seeing
what these eyes first opened for.

What We Really Want

What we really want is not a what
but who, and who we really are
is not a who but how
we live the moment
we have come to know as now.
If it is your thirst that brings you here,
be glad, rejoice,
if it is the quenching of your thirst,
enjoy each drop,
give voice to the finding
and know that when you have
found your fill,
this beautiful longing,
as it has since the beginning of time,
will begin again.

Reading Between the Lines

I just read this entire book of poetry
and was amazed to discover
that what I wanted to say
never actually made it to the page.
Odd.
I thought I had written it down,
I even have memories of it
late at night, alone in my room,
with only the moon
and a few wolves howling inside me,
but I couldn't find it anywhere.

Gone. Completely gone.

Oh sure, there were lines,
but they were more like those you find in a bank,
lines that barely moved, filled with fidgeting people.
I think somebody must have stolen them
when I was out to lunch.
The good lines were definitely gone,
though I did manage to find a few
interesting *spaces* in between the lines,
really good spaces, open spaces,
spaces that seemed as if
they were just about to be filled
with what I really wanted to say,
you know, the good stuff –
like the moment when your child,
thrilled you have finally returned home,
runs headlong into your arms.

It's Your Turn

Ta da! Now it's time for you to write! If poetry isn't your thing, no problem. Write prose. If prose isn't your thing, draw something or make a list. If you want to share your expression with me, it's easy to do. Just rip the page out of this book and mail it to me (Mitch Ditkoff, 268 Main St., Apt #2, Catskill, NY 12414, USA.) Who knows? Maybe I'll publish it on my *Unspoken Word* poetry blog? In the meantime, enjoy yourself. Life is a gift. Open it!

ABOUT THE AUTHOR

Born in Queens, New York in 1947, Mitch Ditkoff has been writing poetry since the age of 15 – ruled by a deep need to express the ineffable.

He sold his first poem to *Rolling Stone* in 1970 for $10 (see page 77). His first book of poetry, *Beggar for Your Love*, was published when he was 50 followed by *Thirst Quench Thirst* and *Full Moon at Sunrise*. The book you are now holding in your hands is his fourth book of poetry and includes 45 of his favorite poems from his first three books and 55 new ones.

He is also the author of three books on storytelling: *Awake at the Wheel, Storytelling at Work*, and *Storytelling for the Revolution* – two of which have won Axiom Book Awards.

In addition to his writing pursuits, Ditkoff is also the Co-Founder of three consulting companies designed to unleash brilliance and the entrepreneurial spirt: Idea Champions, Sage Catalysts, and Face the Music. Over the course of his life, the author of this book has been a dishwasher, busboy, waiter, house painter, gardener, mason tender, bookstore clerk, cook, daycare teacher, social worker, community organizer, subway clarinet player, free-lance writer, political speechwriter, underground newspaper editor, workshop leader, innovation consultant, business owner, keynote speaker, coach, and mentor.

He is the former husband of the extraordinary Evelyne Pouget and the father of two amazing human beings: Jesse and Mimi.

ACKNOWLEDGEMENTS

Massive thanks to the following people whose love, support, friendship, inspiration, humor, kindness, feedback, and patience have kept me diving deeper into what life is all about.

Prem Rawat. Meher Baba. Gurumayi Chidvilasananda. Morihei Ueshiba. Evelyne Pouget. Jesse Ditkoff. Mimi Ditkoff. Barney Ditkoff. Sylvia Ditkoff. Phyllis Rosen. Dina Schwartz. Lori Dahan. Ali Laurens. Spider Duncan Christopher. Ron Brent. Barbara Bash. Joan Apter. Scott Cronin. Val Vadeboncoeur. Steven Ornstein. Francisca Matos. Stuart Hoffman. Billy Salmansohn. Robert Esformes. Steve Kowarsky. Prentiss Uchida. Gil Hanson. Hugo Hanson. Stevie Ray McHugh. Catharine Clarke. Jonathan Lloyd. Steve Gorn. Ellen Goldberg. Zoe B. Zak. Eli Hans. Joseph Bennett. George Fleming. Larry Lefkowitz. Hudson Talbott. Jay Lesenger. Jean Paul Peretz. Sharon Jeffers. Jon Jeffers. Carl Frankel. Paul Alexander. Cary Bayer. Barbara Bayer. Paul Kwiecinski. John Horton. Christine Summers. Eve Baer. Mark Appleman. Charles Cameron. Paul Solis Cohen. Maria DeFranco. Nathan Brenowitz. Laurie Schwartz. Mary Anne Erickson. Richard Erickson. Jan Bernhardt. Warren Bernhardt. Elise Pittleman. Steve Pittleman. Doug Stuke. Aaron Barr. Audrey Philpot. Fazeel Arain. Rahat Arain. Jan Buchalter. Beverly Nelson. Michael Bartlett. Gail Larsen. Steve Wehr. Hank Alpert. Barry Birnbaum. Ellen Greenberg. Roberta Wall. Eric Reinemer. Tim Gallwey. Joe Belinsky. Nancy Seroka. Ted Chadwick. Peter Blum. Eva Snyder. Booth Dyess. Ibi Hinrichs. Tim Moore. Abbey Semel. Ron Frank. Mirtha West. George Samuels. Craig Kluwuhn. Fuzzbee Morse. Tim Hain. Julian West. Kurt Krueger. Susan Gregory. Jim Hobbs. MaryJane Fahey. Alaya Love. Susan Hubly. Lynnea Brinkerhoff. Bill Stevenson. Peter Buettner. Alla Rogers. Paddy Noble. Phil Noble. Alan Roettinger. Marcia Roettinger. Dennis Rosen. Anne Krauss. Mark Nevins. Susan Glass. Tina Lindgreen.

FOLLOW-UP RESOURCES

Websites
- UnspokenWordBook.com
- MitchDitkoff.com
- IdeaChampions.com
- SageCatalysts.com
- FaceTheMusicBlues.com

Blogs
- Unspoken Word: www.ideachampions.com/poetry
- Heart of the Matter: www.ideachampions.com/heart
- Heart of Innovation: www.ideachampions.com/weblogs
- Storytelling at Work: www.ideachampions.com/storytelling
- Medium: www.mitchditkoff.medium.com
- Huffington Post: www.huffpost.com/author/mitch-305

Books on Amazon
- Unspoken Word
- Full Moon at Sunrise
- Storytelling for the Revolution
- Storytelling at Work
- Awake at the Wheel

About Prem Rawat
- PremRawat.com
- TimelessToday.tv
- Youtube.com/premrawatofficial
- TPRF.org
- WOPG.org
- IntelligentExistence.com
- RawatCreations.com

Contact: mitch@ideachampions.com

CPSIA information can be obtained
at www.ICGtesting.com
Printed in the USA
BVHW090019280423
663158BV00019B/743